C000071485

A Speaker for
the Silver Goddess

– Stride –

Other Stride books by the author:

Sheen
What the Black Mirror Saw
Orchard End
Abyssophone
The Laborators
Dressed as for a Tarot Pack

i.m. Peter Redgrove:

Full of Star's Dreaming: Peter Redgrove 1932-2003

The Peter Redgrove Library:

1. In the Country of the Skin
2. The Terrors of Dr. Treviles
3. The Glass Cottage ★
4. The God of Glass ★
5. The Sleep of the Great Hypnotist
6. The Beekeepers
7. The Facilitators
[★with Penelope Shuttle]

A Speaker for
the Silver Goddess

Peter Redgrove

for Don,

love

Penny

x

A SPEAKER FOR THE SILVER GODDESS
First edition 2006
© the estate of Peter Redgrove 2006
All rights reserved

ISBN 1-905024-16-9

Cover design by Neil Annat
Cover art © A.C. Evans 2006
Used with kind permission of the artist

Acknowledgements
*The Times Literary Supplement, Stand,
Poetry Review, Poetry London*

Published by
Stride Publications
11 Sylvan Road, Exeter
Devon EX4 6EW
England

www.stridebooks.co.uk

Contents

Peter Redgrove 1932–2003

Scrotal Education

(Colloquy with a Wizard)

I.

He has laid

the streaming of his cloak

across my shoulders,

The live cloak, the trysting garment,

the robe of ermine invisibility,

of nether powers,

His Spanish cloak of words

seasoned with warm and scrotal breath

like innumerable kisses –

This pyrosome, the female firesnake

Laid in the ermine, seasoned with drink.

II.

Losing the skin's permeability, losing

the sense of the ermine field, to restore it

he laid his bloom

Across my shoulders, pressed

his hat upon my head and its

perspiring band like a round magnet

Tingled like a voodoo silk opera hat

topping off the voodoo dressing-gown

full of eyes; that was the time he

Sank under the oak table screwing with his lady
                into the ermine field waving farewell
                        from under the drinking table,
Buried for then, like Merlin in his oak.

III.

He recalled for me the personage
                in Rabelais who spreads his scrotum
                      like a Spanish cloak
Over the kitchen table
                and sets about scrubbing it clean,
                      his breath horsey
And wholesome, his embrace
                scrotalised, tabernacled, perfectly relaxed –
                      the wrinkled domino between us
Like a map of magic with watercourses and ravines
                as his body drew up over itself
                      the capabilities of a perfect
Astral scrotum invisible to most,
                heaving up the heavy unseen skin
                      and fastening round our shoulders,
The supreme teaching aid, a high-collared mantle
                for two – that he could turn
                      his wedding-tackle into a whole embrace
In pure friendliness!

IV.

To enter with the transparent man
                the scrotal invisible embrace
                                perfectly relaxed within
Like wineskins
                of supple calf containing
                                fluid and bones or rocks
And gently drumming water.

V.

The pub like all the pubs round here
                played its part with atmosphere,
                              this being the Royal Oak,
That is, the Real Oak, lined with ancient timbers;
                being the chief world-being
                              at this time of year
Only their ermine is green, and the small but real
                oak-flowers; we visit
                              both places at once
Inside and outside deeply grained, nothing less
                than the world's scrotum flowing
                              visible and invisible at once.

VI.

His breath is winged shapes, his cloak
        like reading in torchlight
                under the eiderdown,
The whole space filled with lanugo in ermine form,
        a foetus of breathing and reading
                the same tune as the cloak
Plays by touch,
        into which beings like moths
                gather vibrating written wings
Like pages of a magnetism
        which is the same force
                on which the stars fly in constellations
Studding their trysting cloak or paradise.

Grandma Rules

The bags under the mourners' eyes
        show that their kidneys are moving them
            slowly into the next world;
Resting from her five-act funeral
        I remembered how when the rain fell
            I entered another mental world;
My grannie was just the visual form
        or mask of the atmosphere
            that tuned the rooms of that house;
Each room caused a different grannie actually,
        bent the mask, recoloured it slightly;
            her skirts blew her about the house;
Now her rain has fallen for the last time,
        opened its doors and she wholly passed through...
            there is another younger
Grandmother attending the funeral:
        she is wearing a magical suit black as night,
            the sheer Vee of her blouse is folded back
On her jacket collar and breathes at me, and watches
        with the pupil of a small pearl tapping
            the base of the throat
In the oceanic scent her collar distils,
        disguised alchemist, her laboratory on her back;
            and the grandmotherly heart
Taps out its massage message

blending all the perfumes which rule
　　　　　　　　　from those skin laboratories
And silk cellars.

Anima of the Neurologist
(from *Nudist Studies*)

She is wading
                    downstream, her legs
                                        feel plunged into
Wonderful materials:
                    the current deepens,
                                        her throat flowers
Like waterlilies.
                    She allows it to push to mount her
                                        like the pressure
Of the dress over the back
                    of the wicked Queen:
                                        this she thinks
Is why the Queen in Snow White
                    wears her high furling collar
                                        like a white lily
Awaiting inseminations;
                    shown this, the Neurologist
                                        merely bends to his soup
And eats it hungrily:
                    'What ails you?' she enquires
                                        in one of his voices,
'What ails you?' her prune
                    stretching towards him.

Butterfly Museum in Bird Sanctuary
(from *The Importance of Museums*)

Hold seed!

      power awakens!

            under the shed-roof

I have met the butterfly-families

      of Judies and Metalmarks,

            Fauns, Palm-kings, Duffers,

Jungle-Glories, Vanessas, Jezebels...

      they are lion-maned birds

            like flying pekinese,

Oil paintings flapping out of their frames,

      birds flayed in flight

            in the same spirit

As the garden peacocks

      with their cascade of eyes,

            their shrill,

Intolerably short mating-calls,

      their great being of eyes

            standing up whole behind them.

Recovery

I.

Jellyfish meat

           as clear as glass,

                      Candlemass Eve,

Her period yesterday;

            sunshine and wind.

                      It is the day

Goddess recovers

            from the birth of the year,

                      reassembling her own

Body of light; it is time

            to unveil her image on the stair,

                      to go to sleep

Praying for the images

            to answer the prayers;

                      beneath the skin the stairwell

Of the inward senses

            brimming as the moon brims to the full.

II.

A creature that beats its wings and screams

            and grooms itself; elsewhere a person;

                      virility becomes audible

in the voices of magpies and women

who are inweting, and this brings
the clouds to their point
So rain falls... for the women
have been drifting about
in stasis like great
Swollen clouds that cannot
quite release their loads, the men
absolutely bewildered
And staring upwards. Now the air
is full of yonidrops
which settle
Into broad puddles: into these mirrors
Nature peers to glimpse her images
and the magpie in the downpour
Gives an Avesta with her tongue.

Up, Bad Dog!

Like the lion in his roar of rage
  the sky gaped audibly,
    the solar furnace
Opened its doors.
  The heat
    and the African wind,
They are ungraspable, ungaugeable,
  inexpressible
    except through the animals
Which are their equivalents,
  their sensible equivalents.
    Up, bad dog!
Be thy face
  the gaping sky!
    Be thy howling
Thunderous!
  The long-protracted scream
    of those jackals
Succeeding immediately the dawn
  is like the thunderclap rolling
    after the flash of lightning.
Hence it is the earth that is worshipped
  and its mirror
    in the stars
That make invisible existence
  apparent

as the Moon rises
To the howling of ape
who is the voice of that unknown,
a speaker for the silver goddess,
And the animal type
of the calm breathing power
and of the storm-fiend.

The Ayenbite of Inwet

Outness or the vaporisation
          of myself, the mist within
                    that rooms itself

Into steps like pages,
          'a cloud that speaks or sings',
                    a gust lifts the house,

Recaptures the power;
          having hoped to be relieved
                    from a depression by the wind

The impending rain falls
          while the urban poets cannot understand
                    these struggles or submit...

As for the presence of a loved one's
                    internal fountains...

While in the clairvoyant's house
          all the mirrors deepen
                    as the spirits enter

And this is shining inwet, simultaneously
          exhaled steroids and
                    spiritual children.

Caesarian Daughter

Her hands flutter
        round her weeping face
                like trying to tear
Veils off; happy again
        she dances, and prances fresh veils
Building a palace of scarves.
        The surgeon from Africa
                cut into her Mother,
Lifted the Daughter
        through her sanctuary wounds,
                now she tears the veils weeping,
Or rebuilds that sanctuary by dancing
        to build an inside outside
                with invisible walls
Turning columns
        of gestures and fragrances
                mistyknotgardens,
And pleasuremazes, troupes
        of sisterly inpalpable presences dancing;
                there's no more room here,
Out into the garden! across the lawn
        treading elixir out of the blades
                under veil-palaces of the clouds
Until a blackness puts the clouded blue aside,
        tears down the palaces
                in torrents of utterment.

Christmas Father

A magic Yule:

> The women and their children
>> are excited by their presents –

Like one beast, the composite
> Christmas Monster in the straw,

The sparkling pine-tree adds its dimensions,
> in its pyramid of needles,
>> compounds with their perfume

As under the skirt
> of the fairy-goddess at the tip.
>> Santa dressed

Like a winter battlefield passes
> parcels from person to person, snatches
>> into his fiery nose

An increment of sweat
> from one, and then the next
>> who as they gasp

'O thank you, Santa,'
> offer this air-kiss which
>> adds up into his lungs

To a total Christmas;
> Father works hard
>> to afford the exact gift

Which gets the most
> filial smell from Sonny:
>> while Mother

In the kitchen does the alchemy
                    that raises juices in
                                        them all,
She provides the sap
                    which makes them smell
                                        like proper sons and daughters,
Who when they tear off the glitter-paper
                    and rip open the boxes, give off
                                        little squirts of envy –
Gas of laser sharpness.

Seven Powers

'Buy me a candle, Daddy!'
               by the Chinese Hand Laundry;
                         a Seven Powers rainbow taper;
Iris Del Arco watched the splash of oil
               unfolding its gorge-de-pigeon
                         out of the black vault
Of a little bridge
             across the muttering throat
                   of the River Frome.
'Such a candle burns
             for a fortnight
                   releasing its powers
In succession via the several perfumes
             of the variously-coloured wax;
                   such an instrument
Controls our chemistry for two weeks...'
             Then after he died,
                   becoming a woman
In a workshirt cleaning brushes,
             the room ablaze with gloss around her,
                   swabbing her hands
With white spirit.
             In a clean room.
                   A Chinese woman.

Drunkenness

'Beauty is when "The many still seen as many becomes one" '
— Coleridge

Drunkenness – the development
        of the dew, this recomposing
               of the two eyes,
Two globes forced apart by anxiety
        becoming one by an act,
               the flattened 2D becomes
3D; information by decoupage,
        the paintings all become solid,
               from the unfolding in half-sleep
Of a four-dimensional form –
        'Around me the whole strength
               of the street swarms...'
The water
        showing in gravure its thousand names.

Survivor

The mummified dead were groomed
        and sat at table – Look!
                the image of God painted,
Rustling and propped up at table
        wide-eyed and amazed!
                One who in the night-time
Found her face,
        renewed her eyes
                that shone with goose-grease,
And disregarding the paperiness of her lungs
        breathed deep into
                her Osirified chest,
The quick eyes running
        like mercury
                in the painted bone:
Her body of matter
        healed without a seam,
                sitting down at feast
With the pink and the warm,
        the portrait laughing.

Initiatory

After this, a particularly holy room
               where one stood in total darkness;
                             a single water-drop
Touched each one of us,
               and if a single water-drop
                             can resound so greatly
Through the whole skin...
               Indifferent, except for my sake,
                             to these tableaux, she who ate
The afterbirth like a devouring harpie,
               like a sow
                             with the seagulls swooping near,
Mewing for the liverish turquoise,
               to restore her body and savour her child;
                             the infinite communion of that!
Reassembled in her perfume now.
               The picture-show
                             leads back to the same place,
To infinite touch, wherein
               the water-drop trained me, and
                             her company and tolerance; now
We all smell of babies,
               mother, daughter, father
                             in one triple fragrance.

A Kiss

Some peculiarities of the foliage
                astonished him.

                                And he gasped at the flowers

And lessons of the thorn.

                'What is the name of these woods?' he asked.

'Tell me!' he begged.

                'I have been touching palaces in in the dark.'

                                He counts, but not in numbers.

He is strengthened by the gravity
                of the garden-ess.

                                He has the roar of prayer

In his voice.

                The obedient lilac folios

                    open to him

Under the broad grey bands of cloud
                that are the wave-crests to the wind,

                            the boundless mazes

Wandering on into solace.

                And the climax of it?

                        That would be plunging

Into the pond and becoming instantly
                another kind of creature...

                    There was no end

To the imagery of the garden.

                In autumn it began to resemble

                    the skin of an infinite snake

Casting off and full
of confused noises and voices.
She had asked the price
At the place of entrance, paid,
and entered the labyrinth
liking its shadiness.
The deep pit of his kiss
full of the imagery of the garden
awaited her.
She had been only
a woman with long hair
cutting a field of onions –
This was her usufruct – now the meanings rose around her.
The kiss created a fine
but eerie mist,
Strangely veiled and shadowed...
They ate the small flat sweet cakes,
the hyacinth a mere comma as yet
At the heart of its layered lair.

After the Funeral

Putting one's mouth to the cold
                sweet flute in the rainy graveyard
                        for the funeral of an
Old woman whose cheeks were cool and fragrant
                to kiss and whose robes always smelled faintly
Of lily of the valley. Afterwards, tea,
                in the huge gargoyle of a house with its armchairs
Of a deep raisin colour.
                I was upset, distressed, but a remark
                        made by my partner
Cheered me. She was staring at the wrinkled chairs.
                        'Raisin,' she said,
'Raisin up.'
                and she giggled, 'Resurrection, a sign!'
                        and waved her arms
Around her head. A distinct odour
                of lily of the valley
                        came from her armpits,
And I wondered
                whether body-smells were inherited.

Mistress Shivers

The spinet declares

   the waters shall be healed

     and be full of fish

Like gardens of flowers

   as the flow-er plays

     and the moths shall carry

All leprosies away on their backs

   on their scaly backs

     with formal magnitude.

We love among the shrubs

   greeting friends

     to the music of spinets

Among the notes that fly

   as the insects do

     into the shrubs

Who are our friends

   at this garden party all dressed up,

     humans

In floral prints among the flowers

   invisible among their friends as spirits

     gathering their perfumes

Under spreading skirts

   to the music of spinets,

     how easily is a bush

Supposed a broad in clouds of perfume

   broadcast like spinet music

                                        pleasured from the flowers
By bees triple-tongueing each instrument
                        invisibly;

                                        is that pink-blossomed tree
Shuddering off clouds of its perfume, Mary,
                                or an Artemisia swived
By attendant bees
                        as Mistress Shivers pleasures the spinet
                                        on spinal keyboards,
Creature of scent and electricity
                        in her floral gown
                                        and symphonies of shudder.

At the University

'The piano, on which you touch
                the cold treble:'
                                the tender and virgin seal
Pervades the house.
                I meet the vice-chancellor
                                in his robes,
I am in my old blue
                dressing-gown;
                                both costumes
Are loose and open;
                much kissing
                                as counter-octopus
To virginal influences.
                Such contaminations
                                come from love,
University love.
                The ruins are haunted
                                by a reasonable voice
Like a cat's and by the smells
                of the mud-pits, the virtual garden
                                where I have seen
Each thing in its own dawn shadow.
                Morning has the air
                                of a dream until
About 5.30. Therefore the yogis

and the monks

begin their days

In the hours smaller than this.

Ancient Well

I.

My central heating gurgles like an ancient well.
    I thought of God tasting himself in all things.
        He was a man bending over a spring
With a wooden ladle in his hand,
    discussing on his palate
        the taste of the young water
For he only is truly old;

I.

Or he was a man amazed by a dish of mercury
    like the trembling mass of electricity
        which the earth contains,
Watching its reflections shiver and settle
    to be set shivering again by a Godtouch, or
        a splash running in bright orbits
to merge again,
    without seam, just mirroring,
        just not, as the tremors
Begin again, almost steady though, does
    Divinity catch a glimpse of itself
        expressed in the
Molten looking-glass?

The Other Orchestra

The musicians all clad decently,
               a rotting figure
                             in the cello,
An odour of hot silk
               out of the shirt-fronts.
                             In the churchyard
An awareness of all the dead
               holding their breath as if to listen,
                             and in expectation
Of the resurrection,
               for the creepy-crawlies
                             wriggling like that cello
Leave the bones behind
               to devise another figure somewhere else;
                             the second orchestra in the pit,
The octet scraping away at the poolside;
               the movement left in the water
                             by the contralto
Doing a bump-jump
               which commands the second movement
                             and on that cue
The water-pages turn which the whole audience enters
               with hardly an extra ripple.
                             Down below
The octet shuts off
               and there is only the bass hum

                         of the pool's greenness

As the players play and swim
                  downwards into its tune
                        with eyes wide,

The theme altered as each player plunges into
                 the water-music, as by tuning.

Situation

Then I began to eat
           of the tree of knowledge
                      so that my eyes were multiplied.

Touched his balls:
           'Nice basket, Sonny.'
                      A new perfume called

'Double Scrotum'.
           She scraped her palate
                      spider-clean.

A flashing-ope of her gardens
           as she passes by
                      with her train of perfume.

The gorge was full of deodars,
           peepuls and kikars
                      and a few great dominating teaks.

Down here, a small reclusive penis.
           The tweedy stones in the bed
                      of the stream,

The teaching stones rattle.
           This morning she also found
                      the beatific gown.

To keep going, another town,
           another priest-tree to be ordained.
                      The miserable comes visible,

And the joyous too.
           A great curtain is lifted.

The great Round and

The feederfellated.

A faint but intense dawn chorus

as though all the birds

Were standing tiptoe on all the twigs

stretched up and singing

their hearts out.

Feasting Laughter

Feasting laughter! How easily
                is a ghost supposed a girl!
                        Clothes

Seen by radio. Trees
                those green skins laying down, year
                        after year,

Bones of wood,
                and at the poetry reading
                        the sweet smell

Of flowery words, the shadow
                of the great sail of secret
                        precepts carrying us along,

The god and the beast
                playing on the stone
                        together, the white stone,

Our reading-stone with its channels,
                the open book with one white page,
                        it performs and sings at us;

Moving the body after viewing such a drama
                creates fresh images over and over
                        which are radio-echoes

Like feather-breaths
                out of a rustling unseen wing
                        flying through

And through our homes and skulls,
                and out again.

Your Bowl

The bones, according to Chinese Massage,
                    are aerials of the right length
                                        to catch cosmic wavelengths
So I polish along my bones
                    and I study with the cat
                                        for alertness to the invisibles,
Those sudden invisible and hearty warmths unwrapping,
                    breathing off an outside wall;
                                        I linger under trees
Who are senior instructors, great
                    shuddering bells of changed perfume;
                                        humans, Jesus said,
Are like trees walking
                    in their branched aromas, and every raindrop
Almond-shaped like the yoni of everyone:
                    but can this man be Jesus,
                                        I caught him pissing in the pond;
Snap up a bargain bronze Buddhist
                    togetherness-bell
                                        whose rim rubbed with a stick
Creates a resonance like yours;
                    for Maharaga, the great emotion,
                                        for Maharasa,
The great juice or joy.

Glad to See You

A mother's body
                at once earth and paradise, fire and star;
                            every child
Shone with the bloody shambles of its birth,
                  the shiner in the living water
                            known to the witches
Of the Middle Ages; they were accused
                of worship of the Great Devil
                        in the form of a huge star
Which descended to their Sabbaths like a bonfire;
                it was the baby foreseen in fact, star-clad;
                        they went out naked at night
To be skyclad in the touch of the whole air,
                star aethyr,
                        and leapt through the flames
Singeing their scutcheons and with song saying
                'I seek that dark world
                        that enriches the visible one,
I seek the enriched light in dark things,
                in the magnetic oils coiling under the moors,
                        the scented cloud
Full of stars that surrounds
                the meeting of friends
                        and pours from their scutcheons
As from these tall bonfires;

essential earth and paradise

leaping through, in the dark,

So glad to see you.

At the Society

(Witch Nostalgia)

There was the mature Dean of Witches
                who gave me an eye-opening kiss.
                                Her lithe soft hand
Was capable of me.
                The secret of Florent:
                                the older ones grow
Luminous with age,
                luminous as milk.
                                She had witch nostalgia:
Weather her concern,
                the Earth honourable and honoured;
                                when fog capped the mountain,
It was her fire,
                and her weird cronies of the woods
                                like the branches
Hummed incantations;
                at noon they bathed and
                                disappeared into their reflections;
And she is the gossyp
                of the forest-king's leafy-speaks,
                                and of the congregation of childhood.
One of those ready-voiced muses, and
                the pound-weight of her bust breaks
                                her shirt open like a fountain
Of hot skin-breath
                as she confides her station.

Aer

The Seraph Hermaphrodite
    can do all that is impossible,
        Aer's flesh is like a new-born
Child's, mobile and mercurial,
    Aer is in intercourse with Aerself;
        Aer dress is invisible
Woven out of perfumes
    and you can see the whole anatomy
        with yoni and lingham
Everlastingly in place, peace,
    Spun of Aer-mingled distillations
        like woodland scenes
Carried implicitly, so Aer
    greets you from Aer's own green glades
        as though the housewalls
Were transparent; and the polished table
        with the roses on it
Deepens like a well as Aer approaches.
    There is no darkness at all
        for Aer, the night breeze
Is a pressure of light
    containing stars
        like flowing balsam
An under white pressure.
    Aer culls Aer's no-clothes which are
        magical atmospheres

Spinning robes from the winds
        and Aer's sweat

                and from the arbous

As the sun rises when all plants
        are rose-coloured

            and stream with elixir.

Ever-Coming

The foetus drunk
        on its own sweat,
                the foetus steeped
in its own piss, drenched
        in the mother's fatty waters;
                insult him as a 'piss-drinker'
And this is to say
        he is the baby of his mother still, a
                prenatal salt-water fish,
Time he got born.
        And when his mother
                died he flung himself down
In the empty bath and cried
        and a little white Jesus appeared
                by spinal sight
At the acupuncture point called
        Ming-Men GO 4, or
                'The Door of Life'
Which lies in between
        the two kidneys; this apparition
                was like a foetus
In shrouding parachutes
        of mother-silk
                and its arms were raised
And its robes Arabian...

(There is another place

                              known to courtesans

Where a person may

          press so softly with the nails

                              that hardly anything

Can be felt yet every hair

          on the body rises up

                              as though the skin

Were a rustling garment

          and the arms were

                              raised to bestow the actual.)

The Gale Chambers of the Vast Nose
Visions during Yoga breathing

I.

Now establish silence

        and an eternal companion

                walks into the silence

And sits down and listens

        and a tear rolls down her countenance;

                the immortals serving

At this table also,

        immortals eating

                mortal bread,

Weeping.

II.

This plasm of mist aches,

        this phlegm in the air

                like a virtual serpent

Shining with its poisons –

        as the snake coils into

                the hairy wood

The birds beat out of it:

        the serpent enters the cave

                at the root of the

Millennial oak:

        the cave fills with light.

III.

Portions of sky,

  each portion with its own bird:

    birdsong apportions the sky;

Guided by songs over

  immense distances;

    three green peaks

On this lovechart;

  local radio makes local magic,

    the sun shines, he buffs

The car to music

  charioted by a petrol

    rubber and steel device:

The birds open their beaks

  and out comes radio

    and brake-song:

A cloud passes by and the traffic howls.

IV.

One who is all the colours at once,

  a toad that shines in the dark;

    they shine

With their copulations;

  wax, wood, iron, silver:

    mementoes of amplexus

As the blessed toads

practice non-penetrative sex
                                        all day, all night,
Shining with their exercise
                    and good poison,
                                mingling their medicines
Over their shining skins.

Grace and Flavour

She is sitting inside a stone
> and writing poetic prophecies
>> in the close smell

Of serpentine and granite.
> Her dress is of scarlet
>> silked chiffon

Tamboured
> with glass bugles and pailletes;
>> today under her guidance

He came into the orange-tree,
> his palms running with orange-oil,
>> and the rain washed

His white blood into the roots,
> per manus domina,
>> by the hand of the lady,

And offers her an orange –
> she bites and the oil runs down
>> over her shining commendations

And the sheen of her bosom tamboured;
> tantric sex
>> in the tiny glittering bedroom

Like a twirling lantern
> all smelling of oranges:
>> one of the flavours,

Possibly the best

penetrating the halls and galleries,

        the orange ghost of the palace;

A house of such magic

      that they will take us all

        for madpersons;

And in the sky above

      a vast dusty cloud

        made of a universal elixir

Smelling of granite, serpentine and oranges

      hangs heavy over

        Hampton Court Palace:

Did I not say

      that this is where we live

        inside the grace and favour stones –

The Energies!

      Soon, some green rain

        will fall, restoring ghost

To all the flower-gardens.

Love Poem

The snail formula of the millennium
                    coiling to us
                                        from the immense planetary intervals
In Snail-Sabbaths,
                    and their whispering wet cloaks
                                        pronounce,
They assemble among the tombstones
                    holdfast together
                                        in blessed amplexus
A moist foot wearing a dry hat
                    archers of Cupid
                                        a grandclockgraveyard
Made of 365 snails
                    its slow wheels slide out for the rain
                                        tombstone as spirit solidified
Written stones of the house of lichen
                    the empty tomb picked up
                                        so the spirit endures
Our inspection
                    churches on wheels
                                        eyes like slender wands
Hedge-sparrows of Forrabury
                    singing their hearts out
                                        perched on snail-hued tombs.
They have given up snails,

the snails are singing back
in crooked moontracks
Shining up the ancient go-slow.

Who is the Higher Penis Here?

I was visiting

the Mother of Wolves

in her firelit cave,

Her sons and daughters tugging

and wrestling around,

but the higher penis

Today, was a quietly-spoken

Victorian scientist

practising spiritualism

With only three ghosts,

he took me elswehere, to

Dr. Jekyll's laboratory

Where intercourse was not only

imminent but eminent too,

and immanent: the cave

Just would not do;

and I felt an invisible flow up

and around my high penis

And the Lady Doctor felt it too,

it was like the pressure of light,

like the chamber

Of a goldleaf electroscope,

crura of the charged instrument

parting legs;

Science was OK as a direct allegory

of the lower penis, rising;

                                          the psychic penis rolling
Clouds of the seminal ectoplasm
                         risen for consultation,
                                           this was the high colloquy
But it was still penis, stiff sage,
                         winking to his two companions, whispering
                                           of doorlocks
Oily with harmonious toil, true science;
                         paractising spiritualism
                                           with only ghost.

In the Same Day

Nuclear flasks wedged on their truck
        as if in their giftbox
                done in white concrete,
Ruffled theatre chocolates; the fillings
        shed their invisible continuous light:
                Curtains!

The Dragonfly
        like stained glass with wings,
                a sequence of panels
Telling over and over again
        an illuminated story,
                a church-crumb,
A coloured thought hovering in the air.
        Monsters ushered by saints who
                are the ones who can see halos:
A crocodile of schoolchildren.

Horse-Ghost House

She sniffed at my chest and said
>I smelt of fruit and trees, bed
>>the trampoline of biological perfumes,

An adult bed. Claw-marks on the mud,
>the illuminated manuscript of birds
>>fletched in arrow-script;

No wine in the house.
>Flower-arrangements fall into place,
>>cordial but explosive dreams,

Walls soft as velvet to your touch
>where the wise politique horse hangs pictured,
>>the thinking, remembering Equus.

It is what you see in the presence
>of the ghost that matters.
>>The swing empty

And almost still, a little
>musical from rust,
>>selfless as any animal;

Its music carries across to the house.
>The wood-pigeons cooing as if drunk
>>and trying to say 'Hallo!'

The One who sits in her stately
>Chateau D'Eau,
>>the glassy core within

The moving waters, both the nursery
>of unborn children

                                    and the spiral refuge of those
Who are lost or strayed; Who says
                    'Hallow, my friend'.

Shifting

They stopped me with their mass:
                white waterfalls frozen over chalk cliffs;
                      they raised my capabilities
Of playing to them;
                there was an appreciable amount
                      of left hand stride pattern
In the jazz piano.
                The rustling of my shirt
                      shifted like those waterfalls
Over my head like being reborn
                out of a white waterfall
                      or out of the front white door
Of a capacious and electrical house
                of pelting rain, and
                      I called myself 'She'.
She looked into my body and saw there
                two beautiful children playing jazz
                    one was God
And the other was her soul
                and she could not tell at all
                      which was which.

Mirror

Mirror, Spiegel, speculum,
          scukar: shadow-holder.
                    The trance-maidens

With bound eyes
          consult the inner mirror,
                    a mirror that is

Everywhere. The shine
          on polished surfaces deepens, particularly
                    those surfaces that for

The moment are still
          but have been everywhere
                    and respond with images

In the water-surfaces
          (images aquae impressae)
                    by hydromantia...

She listens to a radio play while feeding
          baby, the play and flow of speech
                    creates generous rivers in her,

On a Sony Walkman. Her baby
          smells his meal cooking
                    behind her blouse,

Its shiny surfaces becomes a travelogue.
          The husband smells his dessert simmering
                    between her legs

In the small kitchen
          which, though windowless,

                                        is a fully-equipped planetarium,
They sit down and eat their first course
                    at the mirror-table:
                                        her surfaces
Are clean enough to inspect the moon in.

from *The Life of Water*

I.

The symbol of water
                open to the sky
                              is deceptive, there may be
Thin ice or confusing
                reflections to be mistaken
                              for the thing itself down there
Or it may be full
                of electricity and fish
                              cogniscent of electrical fields
And able to put a bludgeon voltage
                up you, just as Father Heaven
                              manifests a changing field
Resembling verses of the Bible.
                I crouch by this puddle
                          saying my prayers.
In spring thunder
                I believe the life forces
                        care for all;
Thunder approaches like gongs underground,
                green lightning
                              strikes upwards, hissing, stands.

II.

The alchemical chalk
        has life in it.
                The eyewater of the philosopher
Is rinsed out and replaced
        by a finer water, a living brine
                of greater density and magnification,
For the world of tears
        has replaced
                the world of tomes
And the artifex
        with shining eyes admires
                the bones
Of the royal hermaphrodite.
        The descending angel scattered them
                white and lucid –
How they shine
        now his eyes are opened
                and he sees afresh
With the philosophical water in his sockets;
        all pathways seem attractive,
                he has energy,
He will give willing to the fire, to enhance it.

The Count of Some Account

A mass of beard and talon filled the coffin.
One tear was all she allowed herself.
A hush beamed from the cloudless portion of the sky.
She watched the little travelling silence sorrowfully,
Fatal to him.

They were on the high ground of the island where
A little greasy alp parts two peaks; on this coll
The mourners worried their fiddles or with tears on their cheeks
Wept into their hats. Yet that night the unbearded
Count walked, patrolling his battlemented chateau –

It was this habitation was his solid shadow,
And having rebuilt it in his image he could no longer be
Caught in a mirror, his reflection now
Towered on this hill, nor
Caught in a coffin, like the mortal folk,
Nor in the dust, not on the sunniest day: others
Could get lost in his corridors and wander there
Until he chose to let them out or bite them.

The kinswoman thought the funeral was all right
When the parson stopped talking and gave her leave to think
Where the Count might be found; she turned away
And entered the gates, seeking not his shade
But his actual body among the actual stones raised

Into the ancestral home created for her
High up, on the island; he, the soft Count
Beardless, without fangs, talonless, and yet
The Ancestor, the only one, who built
From the beginning for her alone.

Shapeshifter

('I pass through substances. I pierce the darkness. Hidden reptile is my name.
The soul of my body is a serpent of life.'
– Gerald Massey, *The Natural Genesis: II*, p14)

Where light oils the fields,
> the turned furrows almost alight,
>> in a bay called 'Light':

The place where rocks show faces,
> I saw

>> serpents sucking

From black-white cattle as from jigsaws.
> The cliff changing yet the same
>> like the scales of a serpent

Gliding past
> in the pound of the drumcliff.
>> The faces peer

From behind the boulders,
> a gigantic baby with a cliff brow
>> forms out of himself

Sundry serpents with horns and nipples,
> cows laying serpent eggs, incoiled eggs;
>> the cows lie down

Where the serpent basks,
> hidden reptile is his name.
>> A human woman settles

in this cliff's field, and waits,
> she sighs, wriggles in the long grass,

the haunt of snakes and shadows;
She sees into the cave where the rock legs part:
her companion

shapes himself in the sheer cliffs.

Table Talk

At the thin peppermint-chocolate stage
          he was telling us
                  that it was the sea-goddess
Who created the Universe
          out of the Cosmic Ocean
                  in the same way that women
Grow in their brine a secret sharer:
          we were all made of this,
                  star-substance which is baby-flesh;
And how we belonged to a society
          whose members
                  at the solstice deposited
Their semen in rock crevices
          for meditation that made it especially precious:
'Semen is the mortar of the universe,' he declared
          and we drank to that;
                  it smells of briny tempests,
And we drank to that, too.
          Then the Redhaired man, the Man with
                Blood Under his Hat,
Broke in about how the bible
          was a festival of the power of men
                  to become fathers and beget beget,
The woman gave him a long look –
          'No, I am not the Antichrist', he joked

        'but I am a juggler

And a mimic', said the Man with Blood on his Head

      'and as good a storyteller

           as Walt Disney, and, without

Further drink

      told us his personal bible, as he spoke

         we saw how Dagon

Was the grand pantler of the firepits

      where smoke and human steam reflect the flames

         and build a cloud-city

Of human sacrifice lining the horizon;

      and how he entered the woods as Dagon's

        forester and was met

By a Woodmary, the Goddess

    of the wood, through her eyes

       and by his mimicry we saw

The woods recording every wave

    and wavelet, and this was how

       the sea-goddess walked among us,

On the land and through the wood

    as if to say 'burn us, not people, we put

       our learning into the air

For you to inherit; we are never consumed,

    our sayings surpass

      all that we know'.

At that, between the wooden doors

    steps the I Ching as a gracious lady

      and joined hands and this

Ushered in the New Testament of the trees...'
                    'Jesus!' said the seeder of rocks,
                                'if I'm not too drunk,
Teach me to juggle
                    and stand up to Dagon!'
                                'I will', said Rawhead.

Luckbath

'We need the mud'
          – C.G. Jung

Blackening the white garments
                    in order to transfer
                                        their radiance inwards;
Covering himself with estuary mud
                    in order to achieve the inner glory;
                                        clothing the soul
In its shining garment
                    by defiling the outer:
                                        he is changing skins,
He strips the old filth off,
                    the radiant new season begins;
                                        the reek of fruct and filth
Was unbelievable and its look
                    unpredictable,
                                        the monster-look,
The shambler clothed in tree-shit,
                    balsamic cascades,
                                        the body-of-smell reborn;
Nevertheless, the clean twin still visits
                    drawing-rooms, not in his Hyde
                                        but in his snowy Jekyll,
But an invisible forest enters the room too,
                    Hyde concealing himself
                                        in bushes and swinging

From tree to tree;

  silent Hyde; from his seed

    spring great oaks.

The Mistress of Both Worlds

The freight of souls

        travelling by their own ghost-light

                include the grandmother

Younger than himself

        who also lives

                in Lyrical Energy Street

In the midst of her entourage

        of fishponds whose denizens

                leap out into her lap

To have their scales combed

        and hold their water-breath

                sealed behind their gills

Till she has finished grooming them,

        and move at ease

                in her sopping lap.

The Paradise of Storms

Pepper and salt stubble, little
                white crystals mixing with
                                tiny black ones, this crystalline

Scum expounds into its beard,
                the waves of beard
                                flowing out of the skin

Ceaselessly, day and night, registering
                by a small agitation of growth
                                as the trees do

The presence of women
                and the growth-properties
                                of the weather.

Thus the beards, and the trees:
                this one knows that a woman
                                waited under it for an hour today

During the rain; if we took
                a slice of its trunk
                                and looked carefully

At the fattening of the cambium
                which registers the shower we would see
                                a small figure with a furled

Umbrella. In a man
                that would be a barbarity.
                                Can I read that lady

In the unfurling of my beard?
                But the tree-rings should be read

                                    without broaching the bark
For the perfume of a tree
                    compiles its experience
                                    as it matures....
The great detective pauses
                    under the tree full of eyes
                                    in the garden of the murder-house
And the name of the butcher
                    passes into his mind
                                    like a whispering witness,
He lays his hand on the culprit's shoulder
                    whose beard reeks bloody murder
                                    and an *at-last-I-am-caught-and*
Can-rest blend of scents. Now
                    the paradise of storms passes on,
                                    showering in every skin.

Alice's Well

She was a plain
        or standard Alice,
                by no means ugly
Enough to split
        a toad's eyes.
                Falling
Down the well alive,
        thoughts become things
                to be left on the shelves
As she descends. Gossamers
        thrown like a mirror-sheen
                over the old pasture,
She breaks spider-larders
        in the well as she floats
                down. The mad little
Alive (who now lives
        in the barometer) comes out
                with her long shaft
Of mercury, comes out
        and kicks him in the shining shin
                with news of thunder;
The clouds, she says,
        are gathering on the electric wires
                and assembling their messages
On the telephone lines,
        condensing on them and sliding

                              their scenes

Sideways. He was high
                    on the exudations
                                        from toad-licking

As we call it, he saw
                  the mercury fall,
                                        like a well of mirror.

Kiss of Peace

Four winged children
        falling from a cloud,
                a great storm
Blew up from the south,
        broke on the rigid limestone
                eyes in the wooden faces,
The unswathed ones,
        showing their wood-grain
                (Innocence washing her face
Again and again):
        A grim-faced woman
                by the roadside
Scraping the words 'just married'
        off the back window of her car;
                the kiss of peace
Is difficult to obtain,
        especially in a city.
                We met again
Outside Pang's
        whose shopsign illustrated the tale
                of the one-legged man
Who found the two-legged maiden
        in a cave,
                and thought she must be twins.

In the Garden of the Well

The electric blue sky

        has struck its tents

                which lie under the trees

Forming the two bluebell

        syllables *azure*;

                my stuff very glittery,

As glittery as this, like

        a melting blue glass.

                The clouds shatter

Like avenues of noble statues,

        my pint of beer foams

                like a piece

Of good weather swallowed:

        the steps in the well

                called Alice's Tankard

incite to further adventure, underground,

        the witch in each person

                is a piece of the weather,

And her narrative

        like a radiation-badge

                that stains underground,

Or in the sunshine

        clears to azure, meanwhile

                we stay here for ever

Melting our glitter,

watching the well,

listening for footfalls up.

Moth-er

A sudden rose-garden in the bedroom.
                    I pad my way

                                        through this labyrinth
To where she is.

                    As we kiss and touch our quick

                                        windows open to the sky,
Which signal to her, finish.

                    Every dusk she eats a moth, it is

                                        a winged key to the invisible,
It trembles on her tongue,

                    accepting her

                                        as though she were the night
And the stars would bloom in her mouth

                    when this tiny

                                        giving-of-all was enacted,
By moth-kiss, by moth-death. This

                    was her sin,

                                        she had got her sins down
To this small murder

                    and the eating up of this

                                        little star-map...
Her figure reclining in violin shape,

                    a little bonfire on the tongue,

                                        her dozing body pulses
As though the skin were moths,

                    their tones. She

                                        sees through her skin
With a moth's eye and with
                        its radio tuned to moth-death,
                                        the final broadcast...
Completely insupportable,
                        the quicksilver-flutter,
                                        the burst of rank juice
Like a turpentine, like tasting
                        a painter's brush in starlight...
Which paints stars
                        arranged in their cupolas
                                        like whispering galleries
Crowded with white-faced watchers.
                        She licks this brush for luck:
                                        the stars
Painted across the moth's back
                        reappear in heaven.
                                        Now her skin is soft
As as many moths as she's consumed, fitted together
                        in galactic designs of touch;
                                        this is the secret she gives to me,
The winged jewels built into a temple,
                        with her last breath
                                        as conscious mind and the unconscious
Rush together, and the stench or perfume
                        in her last breath seeks above
                                        its constellation of the Mother,
Moth.

The Immense Dew of Falmouth

'Doorlocks loosened by a harmonious oil', a drop from the

        plane's engine touches water, and a rainbow

                springs across the wet roofs;

Water is the big sister

        and the little sister,

                the immense dew of Falmouth,

Dew 'soaking and seductive',

        visible influence spread on all the roofs,

                the moon bright with wonder,

Moons springing up in every roof.

        A mist now: instead

                of a single moon,

Blossom shining over the sky,

        the bloom like an overhanging village

                of the shining dead

With its buttresses and alleys,

        and every room lit up;

                then the bells start ringing

And the mist clears;

        I look at the tiny dew

                on my hairy sleeves:

Moons!

Nidor of Nine Juices

The blended smell after sex,
          the usufruct in the skin,
                    the orchard
In the skin, or as the rose melts
          its odour with the violet,
                    climbs out of our skin;
It is our invisible child
          who looks out through
                    nine windows times two,
The perfume-casements of our solo chest,
          the access buttons that shine
                    like stars in the hug
Of our shirt enclosing us; the hand
          seen plainly laid across the back;
                    this very marine sex
Is best wallowed in;
          meditating in the yoni of the Goddess,
                    the glisten
Seeps slowly like a blessing
          bestowed from above
                    and covers you with that
Flexible garment of juice,
          sitting on a ripple that is inward,
                    you are then
Gorgeously robed in excitement,

a slow electric waterfall;
                    the pulses shining
Or japa of elixir,
            the tap-tap on the head
                        of clitoral distillates
Of the universes, the white source
            just over the head, the robes
                        soaked in moon-juices.
One lives
            in the whole dome of her then,
                        there are
The movements that tenderly
            apply themselves everywhere;
                        strange countryside,
Lawsuits and penalties swiftly cancelled
            like a grassfire on a mountain
                        and the charred places healing
As though nourished
            by the nine fluids
                        in the rain.

Seeing Things at The Lizard V

Enigmatist

The sprinkler in the dark-bright field,

  the lightbeam passing,

    the lamp's shadow passing,

The rainbow dipping in the shadow

  plainly heard, entering the light

    for its moments,

A glimpse on the ear

  of its watery hiss

    white noise fanned

To its full height in the dark

  or bending back towards the black grass;

    when visible in the beam

Silent and full of colours,

  when disappeared fully audible,

    fanning in and out

Of shadow like a peacock-tail

  or a fin of rain

    loud-speaking in the meadow:

I remarked to my companion

  that all the Good Folk

could shine like rainbows, anywhere,

Manifest in fine rain, utter from bright towers, by their

corposants rescue tall ships,

by Jack-o-Lanterns

Full of their light.

Shit and Spirit

Endless trains of paper ghosts
                of toilet-paper hurrying beneath the houses,
Forests upon forests of stink-pipes
                with their invisible brown garbage foliage;
                                in an emergency she uses her frock
And grins at my disgust, tells me
                to get my shit together, I see it
                                generating the ghosts, wrong winds,
Bad smells, too many tourists
                and the composite stench
                                unfurls its wings over the town –
Suddenly now
                sky leaps upwards, cloud
                                blue-bristles open at its crests:
The dead give up strolling
                among their overturned stones, they ascend
                                into the trees until it's time
To come forth...
                and for every person on earth there springs
                              a green tree of the forest
Which is a spirit-home, a very opulent

habitation, a pleasance achieved

by mixing air, rain and shit,

A papery green dress with a slender trunk;

maggots prepare by eating hard

to win their wings,

And within each maggot seethes

a sweet-smelling forest.

One Wedding, One Funeral

Beware the meat

    in this restaurant, choose

        the vegetables

Which are the flesh transformed...

    Waking from a nightmare of a forest

        every tree of which

Is changed into the coffin

    that could be made of it:

        there is no way out

But through these rough doors...

    if you want very clean bones

        use a chalk-lined box,

Chalk is prime skeleton,

    gives immaculate bones if you have need

        of old bones spotless as porcelain...

His mourning skin all changed to wood,

    glued,

        buttoned up over the head

With nails; the ultimate sleeveless

    suit made of imploded trees; look!

the lady mortician enters the wood,

Bearing kindling, and more grief...

I pause, and rap on the box-from-the copse,

I listen,

The family skin is mine now,

he's in the box,

he is all he has got, taking

His wooden turn in the stuffy waiting-room...

Let the boiler-suit of patches and pockets

be my useful alternative overskin

containing spanners,

Vices, keys, loose change;

very manly oily; let it be

a skin like workshops,

Mews-stables and let the stallions in it

batter with their staves

at the mare's intolerable juices...

Or lead your docile fillies out,

in your boilersuit

oh lead the prize colts out,

The radiant horses in their lidless skin...

Your shirtskin is a tent, vaulted, goffred, frogged
                    like a wedding marquee open to the garden;
                              here are the silk ties
To bow it out, the frills;
                    it seems larger on the outside than within,
                              its blousing like a formal
Garden's fountain swoops into its ruching
                    and there is white-work
                              like knot gardens across the bosoms...
Inside this elaborate confection
                    that images the wedding-cake itself
                              is smooth, warm, creamy
Body-atmosphere
                    as though the bride and groom
                              inside their tent
Had started honeymooning before the banquet.

from *The Importance of Museums*

There lie the sandstone bones

        and the human skull

                one millimetre high,

The incredible shrinking visitor

Under the asylum archstones

        plucked from a pyramid.

                The sun rises like

The monstrous chaos

        of mad musicians;

                you are listening too hard.

The stone grains shine out

        in the slant light:

                she had too many reflections

For one mirror to contain.

        So I left her to it

                and quitted the room.

The bone diminished even as I stood,

        I heard the skull dwindle further;

                he ventures in its company

Into the mirror-worlds of the desert sandgrains

        where he may meet and clasp

                his voluble hosts unto him.

The Wall

He wore those glasses
   as if they were
      the dark-framed grooves

Of a magisterial frown,
   but indeed he was fluttering
      with small lightnings

Of cowardice inside
   because, he said,
      he had seen Death

Like a black skeleton
   riding away
      'How could you have seen

Black bones riding a black horse
   in that total night?'
      'A flash hit the whole

Long valley – I saw not only
   that steed and rider,
      it showed me the white shadow

Greater by far
   of rider and steed
      thrown on the mountain-side.'

'That terrible omen...' I began, but

        he bore down on me

                with that thunderous frown −

'It was an excellent sign! *first*,

        Death was riding away,

            and *second*,

Empty-handed, not needing tonight

        to pluck his armful of souls,

            but merely visiting our midnight,

Not worrying about his kingdom,

        moreover, *third*,

            he allowed us to see him.

Now, he will clothe his skeleton,

        hang lip on his bone face

And a tongue within them,

        and become conversible, revealing

            the mysterious beauties

Of his native terrain, letting us past

        not only to, but back again

            with similar privileges

As for his already-citizens;

        I thought the vision meant:

            'At last

The Wall is down.'

Nude Descending

The Saint has multiplied her limbs,

               every thread of drapery a nerve

                             feeling into each corner of the room

As she descends the stairs, the nude, clothed

             only in her vapours, her great

                       power-sleeves, even

In the banal condominium

             now full of grace felt out

                 by her;

With each fresh step a new set

             of feelers is created, or wings, for her

                   auric fields resemble

The gold grain of a moth-wing;

             if we did not know that here

                       is a nude descending we would believe

We were in the presence of a queen of moths

             and her perfumes which were also light

                 like clothes

And provisional ears and muslin

          radio-dishes. Since

                 this gracious passing-through,

Epiphany, was mediated by the odours

we do not now need

any contrived pomps,

For each breath of air,

each lung-full,

is a palace.

Spring Buveur

The ice above moved off

       to a distance, a sneeze

              tuned the nose.

I was a tree at last, and joined air to earth

       with drafts of my good cider

              as I dumped

Excess electricity on to the tree-roots

       by pissing, and the shower caught me.

              The space where I stood

Under the canopy

       opened like a faucet, and I was foliage

              fitting that place,

The high tension gone,

       my clothes wet as the tree's shower-bath,

              and their insulation gone, the sap

Running all over me through my threads

       and all calm in there,

              green and staring. Hot

Tree-piss of the tree's dreams

       shot into the day and the rain

              descended in its cloudburst

Which was us, ripped cloud, tree, and Buveur pissing

                        for it was late April,

                                        and April here

Commands all kind of weather.

Underneathness

The leaves fluttering

      in the open air, so many

            green rags that they are rich;

Opening to the air everywhere

      so the tatters

            are gracious towers

Of coolness, living robes. Indoors, the slicer

            heaps up pink stacks

Of aromatic ham, and the vacuum cleaner

      harvests the reddish fox-brush dust,

            while, further indoors

Under my shirt-tails

      a minute medallion of shit-stain

            from a fart:

Its tiny ginger shines like gold

      in my sky-blue underpants.

            'The sun that shines in the dark,'

Remarks Satinhammer

      in her name the Source,

            'Somewhere, I am sure,

Liszt wrote piano for this gas, his

priestly silver mane

black with sweat,

His heavenly energy expounded in Grand Pianism;

under his cassock,

horse-farts in a minor key.

My Prince

His name translated meant

        Infant Snow, Babysnow,

                The Japanese Prince;

He was almost a young man, with

        his olive oil skin

                and his charcoal business suits;

I wanted him to be transparent,

        and he was trying, not opaque

              or too Japanese,

Since I was sweet

        on his sister the Princess

                which seemed to be plain sailing

In her mind: it was our uneasiness,

        the young man's and mine, which remained.

                Would he become my friend

or would he stay completely

        a Prince of Blood with no affections,

                I would have liked such

A courtly friend; and what I had to offer, why,

        his sister was sure of what that might be, even

              if I wasn't, and I was to

Marry her; why should the Prince

        suspect us?

                All we did, she and I

Was to sit together in one of the palace

        halls, it was wonderful.

Mystery Tale

After my beloved parents have tasted of Life

      and embraced each other in their bed

           scented by their daughter's

Dreams from the very first,

      that made her cot opulent and her speech

           perfumed by her thought

Carried in its breath,

      and lifting her up, the fragrant one,

           the mother

Full of spiritus, the father

      brimful with great intricate anima:

           the parents' bed

Solid with dream-aethyrs,

      a great chariot of magisterium,

           the lungs caressed

In each others' breath,

      with the secret sharer present,

           the witness

Within the mother

      and the child

           of awesome parents

Like possibilities unplumbed; She told me

                the vision she attended as I was conceived –

                        it was a feeling

That was all fragrance that was

                a lion with wings beating

                        the world's trade winds.

Customs

In the Mishna instructions

        are given to women who make

                unleavened bread, they are

To plunge their hands in cold water

        to prevent the dough breathing

                and hinder it from rising.

It is likewise a law

        that during the Passover no man

                may be allowed to chew wheat

For laying on a wound

        because it sets up a process

                of fermentation on the way

To becoming leavened;

        to draw a pitcher of water you need

                a Discreet or Wise Man

Who will do it in profound silence;

        though any person might be a rabbi;

                and on the other side

Of the Glistening Peaks

        the valleys echo continually

                with the howling

Of these saints

        wrestling dragons

                and showing no discretion,

Skins shining like armour

        with the creatures' fermenting spittle.

Sheen

This last book of Peter Redgrove's is one of his most vital with its vivid cluster of images, bursts of ideas and bubbling energy. Redgrove both invents the wonderful and sees it in the everyday. He is a poet who prodigously celebrates and in *Sheen* he is as inspirational and generous as ever. He reveals and creates. He illuminates, juxtaposes; is the scientist of the surreal. He never wears gloves; he touches everything with his own fingers. We feel it all with the same intensity as he does, delicate and raw. He opens doors by the way he looks at what is round him, books, gardens, water, those he loves. In the poignant 'Spiritualism Garden' he pictures himself 'eating on the edge of death', yet in these poems the pulse is as strong as ever; the images as brilliant and original, the gift as abundant; warm, fecund, it germinates still.

'To dip into his work is to receive the gift of magic, and once you're inside you may wish, like me, to never come out.' Jeremy Reed, *Poetry Wales*

'An inimitable poet of great intellect and imaginative power. His vision of the wonders in which we are living part of a living whole is liberating and life restoring.' Kathleen Raine, *Chapman*

ISBN 1 900152 87 8   £10.00

Orchard End

The poems in *Orchard End* open up yet more magical vistas in Peter Redgrove's apparently limitless poetic house and grounds. His is a spiritual, richly imaginative and inventive art, dancing with imagery like a pond full of fish on a bright day, yet firmly based in the everyday, the here-and-now the author observes and science tries to explain. Redgrove is a shaman, a priest and healer, a seer in whose work what is all around us intimates a more hidden, abundant life. As always water and liquid find him at his best, as in 'The Mortier Water Organ', with its snaking jets and inner fountains, or the puddles and bottled rain of 'Service', a poem beautiful in its sexuality and full of puckish joie de vivre.

ISBN 1 900152 11 8   £7.50

What the Black Mirror Saw

A many-faceted composition of prose pieces that draws the reader into a Merlin's cave of revelation and delight. The partially autobiographical pieces on the creative life are especially rewarding and intriguing. One reads with the attention one willingly gives to work by Beckett, Joyce or David Jones, yet in no sense are these pieces long or difficult. The texts are descriptively evocative and vivid, conjuring up worlds reminiscent of those created by Charles Williams, or by Dylan Thomas in *Under Milk Wood*, yet clearly the author's own: worlds created in Redgrove's magic dream-bag, in which images and ideas are shaken up and re-reveried. They are worlds entered with ease by way of Welsh hills, Cornish hills, Richmond Park, Malvern… or by eating oysters.

ISBN 1 900152 10 X   £8.50

Abyssophone

'Streets ahead of anything else… is Peter Redgrove, one of Britain's greatest unconventional voices. Redgrove's work at first may seem surreal but there is no arbitrary image at work here. His ideas embrace Gaia, world-as-one-living organism, the Jungian vision of the soul and the myth and magic of women as the sensual organiser of the world. *Abyssophone* sees him returning with a brilliant new Stride production while continuing his scientifically observed flight into the mesmeric realms of the unconscious.' – *New Welsh Review*

ISBN 1 900152 87 X   £6.95

The Laborators

'Peter Redgrove has been at work again in his laboratory of the human spirit, alchemising all sorts of matter into gold… In *The Laborators* the "Reader in Water at the University of Rock" as he calls himself in "Enterprise Scheme", shows once again the extraordinary fecundity of his imagination, images reproducing, dividing, proliferating with protean vitality. And he shows too that no one else has the same ability to deal with the weightiest and most elemental themes of birth, sex, nature and death with quite his lightness of touch. With his angels and spirits and depictions of all kinds of energy, Redgrove is as bold and wise as Blake, and breezier with it.'
 – *Stand*

ISBN 1 900152 47 0   £6.50

These books are available, post free, from
STRIDE, 11 SYLVAN ROAD, EXETER EX4 6EW, ENGLAND

or online at www.stridebooks.co.uk